DREAMS

Mind Movies of the Night

★

Mary Herd Tull

Illustrations by
Amy Ning

The Millbrook Press

Brookfield, Connecticut

Published by the Millbrook Press, Inc.
2 Old New Milford Road
Brookfield, CT 06804

Visit us at our Web site: http://www.millbrookpress.com

Text copyright © 2000 by **Franklin Tull, Inc.**
Designed by Dahna Solar

Library of Congress Cataloging-in-Publication Data

Herd Tull, Mary.
    Dreams: mind movies of the night / Mary Herd Tull; illustrations by Amy Ning.
        p. cm.
    Includes bibliographical references and index.
    Summary: Examines, in a question and answer format, the scientific and cultural
aspects of dreams, including such topics as the physiological reasons for dreams, the
connection between dreams and religion, and the dream life of animals.
    ISBN 0-7613-1512-8 (lib. bdg.) ISBN 0-7613-0937-3 (pbk.)
    1. Dreams--Juvenile literature. [1. Dreams--Miscellanea. 2. Questions and answers.] I.
Ning, Amy, ill. II. Title.

BF1091 .C75 2000
154.6'3--dc21   00-020885

Table of Contents

The Way We Dream

Answers to Dream Questions Every Kid Should Know

Introduction

Have you ever opened your eyes in the morning with the feeling that you had just played the starring role in a *very* strange movie? You can't remember who else was in it, what part you played, or exactly what happened. You thought you knew a minute ago, but now you just remember bits and pieces of it. The more you think about it, the foggier it gets. Of course it was a dream. You star in dream movies every night whether you remember them or not. As soon as you fall asleep the theater doors start to open.

For thousands of years people have been fascinated about what happens to our bodies, thoughts, and feelings when we dream. Sleep is something our bodies have to do in order to survive. Now researchers also believe we need to dream in order to be emotionally and mentally healthy. Recent experiments link our dream and sleep patterns to brain activity. Scientists have studied thousands of people as they sleep and have found out many things about how and when we enter the dream theater. Still, no matter how much we learn in sleep laboratories, every night new mysterious dream movies open for each one of us in our private theaters. They leave us with questions in the morning that we may never be able to answer.

Forty Winks:
The World of Sleep

Why do I need to sleep?

How do you feel when you don't get enough sleep? Groggy? Slow? Out of it? That isn't surprising. Sleep rebuilds your energy, recharging both your mind and body for peak performance the next day. If you don't get the right amount of sleep, you're putting your health – and even your safety – at risk.

While your body sleeps your brain stays active. It's freed up from its waking jobs to do housekeeping chores that affect how your body functions. It has time to make repairs to cells, cuts, bruises, and sore muscles. It builds protein and restores control of the nervous system, muscles, glands, and all body systems. It keeps a young body like yours growing by making new cells. Your brain also performs jobs that help you think clearly, solve problems, and remember things. Some researchers believe that during sleep your brain replays the events of the day, sorting through new information and building your memory bank. Its nighttime work might help you create new ideas and find solutions to worrisome problems when you wake up.

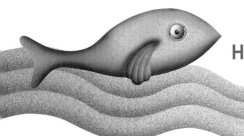

How much sleep do I need?

Some people have wondered why we can't get recharged like fish do, resting for a few minutes every few hours. It would free up a lot of hours that we spend sleeping every night! Getting enough sleep, however, is critically important for your physical and mental health. Sleep experts say to be in a good mood, mentally sharp, creative, and full of energy each day, you will need to spend at least one-third of your life sleeping. Over a normal lifetime that means nearly 24 years in bed!

Edison's Light Bulb

Researchers have found that people need different amounts of sleep at different ages. New babies need the most sleep, requiring about 16 hours each day. By the time they reach age two, children sleep only 10 to 12 hours. Adults sleep an average of 7 to 8 hours. Sometime between the ages of 60 and 70, many people find it difficult to sleep very long. They take more naps but sleep only 4 or 5 hours a night.

Before Thomas Edison invented the electric light in 1879, people slept at least 10 hours each night. After the lights came on, human sleep time got much shorter. In our current hectic life, sleep isn't valued very much. However, scientists now believe that ten hours might be exactly what people really need. Researchers working in areas of northern Canada put away their watches and slept whenever they felt sleepy for as long as they wanted. They quickly settled into a sleep pattern of 10 hours a night.

Recently, doctors have found that teenagers' sleep cycles are different from adults or young children. Because of the hormonal changes of puberty, their internal sleep-wake clock is set differently. They need to go to bed later and sleep later, and require about 9 hours of sleep each night. Teens who don't get enough sleep risk lower grades and even car accdents by falling asleep while driving. To make sure their students get enough sleep, some high schools are considering changing school hours to start and end later.

What would happen if I didn't sleep for a long time?

Some scientists believe that if you stopped sleeping completely, eventually you would die. After even a few days without sleep, you would have trouble remembering things. You would not be able to pay attention to anything for very long. You would make silly mistakes and find that you couldn't solve even simple problems. If you didn't sleep for more than three days, you would begin to confuse daydreams with real life, see things that weren't there, and feel physically sick.

In January 1965, Randy Gardner, a 17-year-old high school student from San Diego, stayed awake for **11 days** while being closely watched by doctors. That's the longest a person has gone continuously without sleep. During that time he felt terrible, lost touch with reality, and thought about frightening things. After he went to sleep again, he suffered no long-term emotional or physical damage.

Modern Schedules - Ancient Needs

People have been on the earth for about 4 million years. It's only been in the last hundred years that human beings have been doing sleep-deprived things, such as working late into the night, pulling all-nighters to study for exams, and watching late-night TV. Some experts believe that our physical, emotional, and mental needs are still tied to the sleep requirements of our primitive ancestors who slept much longer than we do each night.

What does my body do while I'm asleep?

Scientists have been able to learn what happens to us during sleep because of the development of the electroencephalograph, or EEG, a machine that records the brain's electrical signals, or brain waves. To learn about sleep, they ask people to spend the night in scientific laboratories and sleep while hooked up to an EEG machine. Scientists study their brain waves to watch for changes in wave patterns. They also track changes in heart rate, body temperature, and breathing rate. Through these experiments, scientists have been able to tell what changes our bodies go through while we sleep.

During your nightly sleep journey, you go through four different stages of sleep. In the first stage, you get sleepy and fall asleep. Stage two is normal light sleep during which you can be easily awakened. Stage three takes you deeper into sleep. Stage four is the deepest sleep. When you have moved through all four stages, you have completed one sleep cycle. At the end of each sleep cycle, which takes about 80-90 minutes, you have a period of dream sleep. Scientists call this period REM sleep, or dream sleep. During the REM sleep period, your body temperature, breathing rate, and heart rate speed up from their normally low sleep levels.

The Brain's Wiggly Lines

An EEG machine makes different kinds of wiggly lines to record your brain waves. If it recorded all your brain waves for an entire night's sleep, it would produce a piece of paper a half-mile long.

Do I dream all the time I'm sleeping?

When you first fall asleep your brain and body are tired. During the first hour you don't dream. After your first complete sleep period, or cycle, you stay asleep but your brain wakes up and starts to dream. Your first dream lasts about eight or nine minutes.

Dreaming seems to take a lot of energy, because after every dream your body needs to go into another deep sleep period again to rest. Your brain can still produce random dreamlike images during this rest time, but they are less clear and you usually won't remember them as a dream. After each rest period you enter REM, or dream, sleep again. Each dream gets longer as the night goes on. Your brain seems to get more dream-active the closer you get to waking up. The last dream you have can last as long as an hour. By the time you open your eyes and stretch in the morning, you've likely had five different dreams and have been dreaming for two of the eight hours you've been asleep.

Can I learn while I'm asleep?

Many scientists believe that while you're asleep, your brain is busy processing and organizing the bits of information you've collected during the day. It shifts short-term memories into long-term storage and keeps important information from getting lost. This may be why some experiments have shown that people who sleep better have an easier time learning new things when awake.

While researchers believe that the brain is busy cleaning up our memory bin, the part of the brain that stores new memories seems to be shut down while we sleep. That's why we have a hard time remembering our dreams.

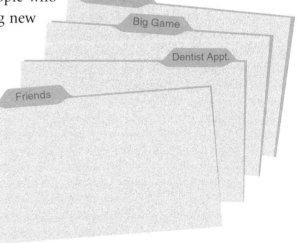

Why do people walk and talk in their sleep?

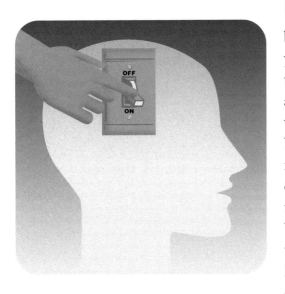

Usually, the part of the brain that lets your body move sets its controls to "off" while you sleep. You may change position during the night, but most of the time you are limp and relaxed. When these controls are not working properly, sleepwalking can happen. Young children, whose brain controls are not fully developed, walk in their sleep more often than adults. Sometimes people walk in their sleep during times of unusual stress. Whatever the cause, scientists have found that sleepwalking is not related to dreaming. People walk in their sleep only during non-dreaming periods and are not acting out their dreams.

Stories about people walking and talking in their sleep can be very funny. There was once a man who would try to iron his pants in his sleep. Luckily, he didn't plug the iron in! However, sleepwalking can be potentially dangerous. Some people have been known to wander around for more than half an hour, walking right out the front door. It's best to gently lead sleepwalkers back to bed. They won't remember anything about it in the morning.

Unlike sleepwalking, people talk in their sleep when they are dreaming and when they're in non-dreaming, deep-sleep periods. They may say single words, whole sentences, or complete nonsense speeches. They aren't necessarily talking about their current dream. Sleeptalking usually comes during stressful periods or times of illness when a person has a fever.

How can I make sure I fall asleep easily?

Millions of people have trouble sleeping. Usually it's because of stress, emotional upsets, worrisome changes, too much eating or drinking before bedtime, or illness. Try these simple tricks to go off into dreamland with ease:

★ During the evening don't drink anything with caffeine in it, like hot chocolate, coffee, tea, or sodas.

★ Try to go to bed and wake up at the same time each day. Develop a regular sleep schedule.

★ Make sure the lights, sounds, and temperature in your bedroom are comfortable.

★ Choose activities at the end of the day that make you feel calm and relaxed. Try taking a hot bath, reading a good book, or listening to quiet music.

★ Don't exercise right before bed. Exercise helps you sleep but should be done earlier in the day.

★ Have a glass of milk. Milk contains an amino acid that may act as a natural relaxer.

★ Don't watch the clock and worry about falling asleep. Just relax. You'll fall asleep when your body is ready.

Famous Sleepers

Thomas Edison only slept 3 or 4 hours a night. (He did take naps.) He declared sleep "a waste of time" and a practice left over from cave days. Comedian Jay Leno manages to get by on 5 hours in a night. Albert Einstein said he needed 10 hours of sleep to function well.

Sleeping and Driving Don't Mix

The National Highway Traffic Safety Administration estimates that sleepy drivers cause about 56,000 crashes every year. Sleep-related crashes are most common among young drivers.

Dream Sleep

What is a dream?

Dreams are unusual stories or movies that you seem to take part in while asleep. They may be imaginary, but they feel real when they are happening. They may be related to things that have happened in real life, deep feelings you hold secret, or completely mixed-up, confusing images and events that make no sense. They can make you feel happy, peaceful, sad, or terrified. After a night of flying over your own house in your teacher's car trying to zoom down and steal your brother's Hawaiian shirt (which you don't even like), they can also make you laugh.

Since ancient times, people have argued about dreams. Is a dream a nightly electrical storm in the brain that gets rid of useless information? Is it a mind movie created for our learning and entertainment? Is it a warning about the future? Today, most people believe that a dream is a tool that helps us learn about ourselves and find creative solutions to problems. As crazy as they are sometimes, dreams may be the way our conscious awake mind learns from our sleeping unconscious mind to help us stay healthy and sane.

Why do I dream?

Scientists agree that dreams are caused by our brain and its activities. Changes in the electrical waves that the brain gives off during sleep show that you are dreaming. Beyond that, researchers have different ideas about why people dream and what they mean. Here are some reasons experts feel we dream every night:

- We dream to fulfill wishes that can't come true in real life.
- We dream to learn about our feelings and fears.
- We dream to find solutions to problems and create new ideas.
- We dream to help our brains sort out the day's events and information.
- We dream to get rid of useless information and clean up the brain's storage bin.
- We dream to take a nighttime movie break from the difficulties of daily life.

13

What does my body do while I'm dreaming?

During regular sleep your brain waves are slow. When you start to dream, your brain waves get faster and smaller. During certain periods of the night, your brain waves are so active that they look like you're awake, but you're not. Your eyes move behind your closed eyelids as if you are watching events happen. Scientists call this *rapid eye movement*, or REM. For this reason, dream sleep is often called REM sleep. While dreaming, your body might twitch and roll over but you can't make any big movements.

What parts of my brain are active when I'm dreaming?

Scientists have used neuro-imaging techniques to trace blood flow in the brain during periods of dreaming. They found that the parts of the brain active during dreaming include those that regulate arousal, emotion, motivation, memory formation, and the ability to process visual and auditory information. The brain areas and functions that appear to be turned off while dreaming are those that enable us to plan, think logically, have a flow of memories that make sense, think abstractly, and receive visual input from the outside world.

Scientists used to believe that the brain stem is the only area of the brain where dreaming originates. In the area of the brain stem called the *pons,* a chemical change is believed to trigger most dream activity during REM sleep. However, research has identified activity in the forebrain area during dreaming. Many scientists now believe that dreaming can be started by different parts of the brain and that people don't just dream during REM sleep periods.

How many dreams do I have during the night?

After age six, you dream about two hours every night. During that time, you probably have five different dreams. A dream can last anywhere from 5 minutes to more than 30 minutes. A dream isn't a fast-forward movie. Your dream activities take the same amount of time as they would take if the events happened in real life.

Can things happening around me change my dreams?

You can be affected by things going on around you while you're dreaming. Experiments have shown that if cold water is gently sprayed on your face while you're dreaming, when you wake up you will likely talk about water in your dream. If you hear a noise or smell a strong odor, that noise or smell will likely appear in your dream story.

Why can't I always remember all my dreams?

It's hard to remember your dreams, some scientists believe, because the part of your brain that stores new memories isn't operating while you're dreaming. Some experts have concluded that dreams are the way the unconscious mind gets rid of information it doesn't need or want to keep. It's information that should be forgotten. It's also true that if you wake up during a non-dreaming period, you are unlikely to remember any of the night's dreams. The best chance you have to remember a dream is to wake during a dream period, lie quietly, and think about the dream for the first ten minutes you're awake.

Why do I sometimes have the same dream more than once?

If you believe that dreams have meaning, a dream that you have more than once may point to a problem, feeling, warning, or lesson that you need to think about. It keeps coming back to get your attention.

Different Dreamers — Different Dreams

Will my dreams change as I get older?

You dream less as you get older. Newborn babies spend half their sleeping time in dream sleep. Researchers believe that babies sleep and dream so much because it helps them develop and learn. By age six, you spend only 25 percent of your sleeping time in dream sleep. That's approximately the same amount of time a grown-up dreams. As you get older your dream stories become more complex, because you have had more experiences and can think about more interesting and complicated things.

Do girls and boys dream about different things?

There have been many studies about the ways the dreams of boys and girls and men and women are different. Researchers wonder whether these differences are caused by our biology and genes or by the different ways our culture expects boys and girls to act. The dream images below can occur to both sexes, but are more common to one or the other. What do you think?

Girls	*Boys*
Many people, both girls and boys	Fewer people, mostly boys
Relationship stories	Action stories
Animals/pets	Sports
Houses	Machines
Indoors	Outdoors
Clothes, jewelry	Tools

Women	*Men*
Remember their dreams more often	Remember fewer dreams
Indoor settings	Outdoor settings
People and relationships	Fewer people, mostly males
People they know	Strangers
Family	Action, running and jumping
Babies and children	Protecting something or fighting

Do my personality and interests affect my dreams?

Researchers have found that your personality can affect what you dream about. Dream expert Rosalind Cartwright believes that "we're as much like ourselves in sleep as we are when awake." For example, dreamers who are outgoing and involved in a lot of activities have more people in their dreams than dreamers who are shy.

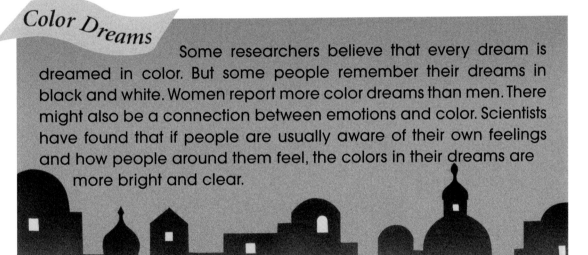

Color Dreams

Some researchers believe that every dream is dreamed in color. But some people remember their dreams in black and white. Women report more color dreams than men. There might also be a connection between emotions and color. Scientists have found that if people are usually aware of their own feelings and how people around them feel, the colors in their dreams are more bright and clear.

Do some people never dream?

Everyone dreams, but not everyone remembers their dreams. Sleep researchers have found that some people forget their dreams more quickly than other people. They may even claim that they never dream, but they do. Since we know the memory-storing part of our brain isn't active when we dream, it usually takes extra work to bring dream experiences into our waking minds.

Do some people have the power to control or change what happens in their dreams?

Dream researchers are interested in the power of people to change what happens in a dream. When you're dreaming and know that you are dreaming, experts say you are having a *lucid* dream. Stanford University researcher Stephen LaBerge believes that when you know you're in a dream you can learn to control what happens. You can even change the story in a nightmare from something scary to something pleasant. Once LaBerge dreamed he was climbing one of the tallest mountains in the world. It was windy and cold. He looked at his arm and saw that he was wearing only a T-shirt. He was afraid that he would freeze to death. Suddenly, he knew he was dreaming. He decided to control his dream, so he raised his arms, jumped up, and flew off the mountain.

Dream Test

Lucid dream researcher Stephen LaBerge says that there are ways to check to see if you are dreaming or awake. Focus on an object and then look away. When you look at the object again and it has changed, you can be sure you're dreaming.

18

Nightmares

You find yourself turning a dark corner in a strange city. You hear heavy footsteps moving faster and coming closer behind you. When you look back, you see an enormous slimy creature that keeps changing colors. It has a knife. You hear yourself cry out and you wake up with a start. It's the middle of the night and you're in your own bed. Your heart is pounding and you're terrified. Tears start to fill your eyes, and you feel like running for the nearest grown-up's bedroom. You can't decide if the monster you just saw was real or not. Don't feel alone. You've just had a bad dream, or a nightmare. Everyone has them.

What is a nightmare?

Nightmares are frightening dreams that seem very real. They leave people feeling shaken and upset when they wake up. For some reason, children have more nightmares than adults. They usually happen in the last several hours of sleep and can cause the dreamer to wake up suddenly. During a nightmare, the dreamer may see horrible people, terrible monsters, or wild animals. Sometimes everyday objects or situations become strange and twisted. The dreamer may feel that he or she is falling or is being chased. Dreamers may remember the details of a nightmare for days afterward or forget them if they fall back to sleep and dream a new dream.

Why do we have nightmares?

No one is sure why people have nightmares, but most people have them. We all have similar common nightmare experiences of waking up in a cold sweat from being chased or trapped or from experiencing a terrifying fall into the darkness. Some researchers believe that nightmares are caused by fears, frustrations, and problems that worry us while we're awake. When kids are worried about school, relationships with friends or family, or big changes in their lives, they seem to have more nightmares. People who have had a terrifying experience, such as a car accident, an earthquake, or a fire, often have nightmares that replay the event.

If I have a nightmare, what does it mean?

Researchers and scientists disagree about what any dream means. No one knows for sure. It's certain that what happens in a nightmare shouldn't be taken as a real-life event. A slimy monster is not really chasing you around your neighborhood. Maybe the heart of its meaning is the *feeling* you have during and after it. Questions you might ask are about your own worried thoughts and feelings during your waking day: What is troubling me? What worries are chasing me and won't let go? What doesn't feel right in my life right now? During a dream our minds let down all the usual walls, and fearful, anxious feelings can sometimes play out in a scary and confusing horror movie. It might be just the mind's way of getting rid of thoughts and feelings that it doesn't want to keep any longer. It might also be a reminder to face and deal with a problem.

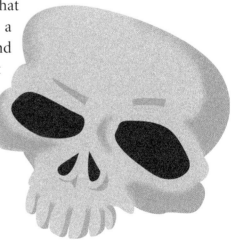

Exercise May Prevent Nightmares

Researchers from the University of Arizona College of Medicine conducted a study about nightmares. They studied the nightmare patterns of 400 women. They required one group of women to walk at least six blocks a day. The other group did not walk at all. The women who walked daily had about a 75 percent lower incidence of nightmares than the women who didn't exercise. Researchers believe that exercise lowers stress and anxiety, both of which seem to bring on nightmares.

What if I dream about death?

Scary dreams are never exactly what they seem, nor do they mean something bad is going to happen. Dreaming about someone's death, even your own, does not mean death is around the corner. It might mean that your feelings for that person are changing. It might mean that you are worried that the person doesn't like you. A death dream could mean you are experiencing an important change in your life. Maybe something that you used to count on is dying. It could even mean that you are worried about your own safety.

Dreaming that bad things happen to people you know and care about can make you feel guilty, especially if you are the person in the dream who is hurting them. Maybe you were angry with your sister when you went to bed. You dream she dies after you push her out an open window. This is likely your mind's way of letting off steam. It's nothing to feel scared or guilty about.

If I dream I am falling, will I really die if I land?

People have a lot of scary superstitions about dreams like this one. During nightmares people often dream they are falling. It's a good example of how our feelings of anxiety and fear express themselves in bad dreams. Who wouldn't feel anxious falling out of a building? Yet though we have the scary feeling of falling, people usually don't dream to the moment of landing. Even if they did, they would not actually die at that moment in their dream. They may wake up with a start, however. So many people dream about falling that some scientists believe it comes from our days when we were toddlers learning to walk and falling down all the time.

What if I dream I can't move?

Sometimes during a nightmare you feel paralyzed, unable to move and escape the danger that's coming. It's a terrifying feeling. You might even find yourself trying to move a part of your body in your dream to make yourself wake up. This feeling of fear and helplessness is often part of a nightmare. Scientists have found that the part of our brain that controls movement actually shuts down while we are dreaming, perhaps to keep us from actually running out of the house during a nightmare.

Will I have a nightmare if I eat pizza before going to bed?

You might have a scary dream if you eat a lot of anything too late in the evening. If your body is hard at work in the middle of the night digesting food, your brain also has to be more awake to do the job and might produce more active dreams. Sometimes, nightmares are caused when something is physically wrong with our bodies. Maybe you're feeling smothered or too hot in the blankets. Maybe you're thirsty. Maybe you have a fever. Maybe you have eaten too much pizza and have a stomachache.

How can I make myself feel better after a nightmare?

One way to feel better after a nightmare (without waking someone else up) is to replay what happened and change the parts you don't like. Create a new script for the movie. Face that slimy monster and turn him into a squeaking mouse with a wave of your hand. Come up with a new ending that makes you feel happy and relaxed enough to go back to sleep again.

Night Terrors

A night terror, or sleep terror, is not the same as a nightmare. When you wake up screaming and confused but can't remember anything about the dream that terrified you, it was a night terror. Night terrors happen during non-dreaming sleep.

The Dream Life of Animals

Do animals dream?

Have you ever watched a dog quietly sleeping in the corner when suddenly, he starts whimpering, growling, and moving his paws? He's in REM sleep and probably dreaming. If you wake him, he might look a little confused, just like a person coming out of dreaming sleep. Scientists believe that many types of animals have active dream lives. This is because their brain waves show different patterns during sleep, including the pattern of REM sleep, just as humans do. Their eyes also move behind closed eyelids, another characteristic of REM sleep. Like young children, young animals appear to dream more often than animals that are fully grown.

Sleep Pictures

Animals can't talk, so it's hard to know if they really experience dreaming. However, one morning a gorilla who had been taught sign language put together two signs to form the term "sleep pictures."

Are there any animals that don't dream?

Scientists have observed that a bird's brain waves show a slight possibility that they have a dream period. However, invertebrates (animals without backbones), such as reptiles, insects, fish, and frogs, do not show evidence of dreaming. They rest rather than sleep, experiencing quiet periods when they don't seem to be aware of what is happening around them.

How often do animals dream?

The frequency of dreaming in animals seems related to body size. The smaller the animal the more frequent the active sleep or dream periods. A mouse has a dream every 9 minutes. A cat dreams every 15 minutes. Monkeys, like human children, dream every 50 minutes. Gorillas and adult humans dream about every 90 minutes.

Standing or Lying?

Sometimes position has an effect on animal dreaming. Cows and horses sleep while standing up, but for some reason they dream only while lying down.

What does the ability to dream have to do with brain size?

Jonathan Winson, a New York neuroscientist, believes that the ability to dream might have helped mammals to develop smaller, more efficient, brains. When the first animals appeared forty or fifty million years ago, the ability to dream allowed them to update their waking experiences. They could match old and new memories and rehearse what they might do in new situations. Like a computer, this off-line brain processing that happens in dreams made it possible for these evolving mammals to become smarter without needing enormous brains.

Dreams Through Time

Introduction

Who had the first dream? Was it a *Tyrannosaurus Rex*, sleeping soundly after hunting down an unsuspecting plant eater? Was it a hairy ape, exhausted after a day of searching for food? Was it an early human, dozing in a cave by the fire? We can't be completely sure. Scientists suggest that REM sleep, the stage of sleep connected to dreaming, probably developed in early humans about 130 million years ago.

No one knows when people began to think about their dreams and share them with others. Some researchers believe that ancient cave paintings and rock drawings might contain pictures of things that early people saw in their dreams. They guess that the people who told the world's first stories might have mixed together things that happened in dreams with events that happened in their waking world.

It's certain that dreaming opened the theater door of the unknown to every dreamer. Researchers who study the things left to us by ancient peoples believe that, for our ancestors, there was little difference between a dream and a message from supernatural powers. It is not surprising that in most world cultures, dreams have been connected to religious beliefs.

Modern scientists have learned a lot about what happens to us physically when we dream. But *why* we dream every night and the *meaning* of our dreams remain a mystery. After hundreds of years of studying dreams, scientists and dream experts have many different theories. What is certain is that throughout history dreams have entertained, confused, frightened, and inspired people. In some cases they have changed the world.

Dreaming in the Ancient World

Mesopotamia (7000 B.C. – 539 B.C.)

The dream stories of Mesopotamian kings from 5,000 years ago have given us our first clues about the dream lives of ancient peoples. Since rulers were believed to be close to the gods, their dreams were very important. Where the dream happened, what it was about, and what it might tell about the future were noted in royal dream reports.

The Mesopotamians believed that people could communicate with the gods only in their sleep. Everyone wanted to receive an important dream message from the gods. The practice of *dream-seeking* (dream incubation) developed. Since the closest a person could get to a Mesopotamian god or goddess was their temple, people went to sacred temples to sleep and to wait for dream messages. Sometimes they stayed for days praying for a dream, especially one that contained good news.

Special priestesses helped Mesopotamians understand their dreams. They told them what different dream images and events meant for the future. If a dreamer met a bird in a dream, it meant something lost would be found. But if a dreamer was flying in the dream, he or she would soon lose everything.

Getting Rid of a Dream

No one likes bad dreams, including Mesopotamians. To get rid of a nightmare, a Mesopotamian dreamer would tell the story of the bad dream to a lump of clay and then throw it into the water to crumble and disappear. If that didn't work, the dreamer might share the nightmare with a blade of grass, and then set it on fire until all that remained was ashes and smoke.

Ancient Egypt (4000 B.C. – 332 B.C.)

The ancient Egyptians, like the Mesopotamians before them, believed that dreams were messages from the gods and important in predicting the future. Since the pharaoh was considered a child of the sun god Ra, his dreams were of special importance.

Serapis was the Egyptian god of the underworld and oracles. There were many temples where people could worship him and spend nights dream-seeking. People trained to interpret dreams lived in the temples to help people understand the meaning of their dreams. One sign that archaeologists found on a temple door stated: *I interpret dreams, having the gods' mandate to do so. Good luck. The interpreter present here is Cretan.*

The Egyptians also thought of ways to dream-seek and share dreams from a distance. If people couldn't get to the temple, they could send someone in their place to dream on their behalf. If they wanted to cause a friend to dream, they could write down a dream prayer for that person and put it in the mouth of a dead cat. Egyptians believed that cats, dead or alive, were sacred and powerful.

The earliest known collection of dreams was written in Egypt. This ancient dream journal described 143 good dreams and 91 bad dreams. Seeing a large cat in a dream was good, because it meant that the dreamer's harvest would be large. Catching a bird in a dream was bad, because the dreamer would soon lose something of value.

Put Bes Over Your Bed

The Egyptian dwarf god Bes protected people's houses from evil spirits and nightmares. Archeologists have found drawings of Bes over ancient Egyptian doorways and on the headboards of Egyptian beds.

Ancient Greece (2000 B.C. – 146 B.C.)

The people of ancient Greece believed that dreams were stories from the gods that could tell them about the future. They studied them carefully and had a complex system to describe what dreams meant. The Greeks produced the largest dream dictionary, *Oneirocritica,* that has survived from the ancient world. Its author, Artemidorus, collected five volumes of Greek dream interpretations. He wrote separate meanings of the same dream for people with different jobs, family situations, and religions. For an Egyptian priest, dreaming that your head had been shaved was a positive sign, but for a sailor it meant that a shipwreck was likely to happen.

The Greek people enjoyed going to the theater. Greek writers like Homer used dreams in their plays and poems to send messages from the gods to important characters. A hero's dream often changed his life, bringing good or bad fortune. However, Homer didn't believe that every dream was a true dream. Sometimes characters had false dreams that caused surprising twists in the story.

The Greeks believed that dreams were connected to a dreamer's physical health. Dreams were a source of healing. Hippocrates, the father of Greek medicine, believed that if a dream showed all the stars shining in their correct positions in the sky, the dreamer's body was in good shape. If a star was out of position, it was a sign that something was wrong. Dreaming of overflowing rivers meant that the dreamer had too much blood. Hippocrates also believed that the way our bodies changed from sleeping to waking was caused by changes in body temperature. He suggested that when people feel sleepy their blood is cooling down.

Dreams for Healing

The Greeks sought healing dreams from Aesculapius, a Greek healer who after his death came to be considered a god by the Greek people. They would go to shrines or temples dedicated to Aesculapius and request a healing dream to rid them of illness and pain. If they were lucky, Aesculapius would appear to them in a dream to tell them which medicine they should take. The symbol of the snake was the emblem for Aesculapius, and in many of his temples snakes crawled around on the floor.

The Romans

The Romans borrowed most of their beliefs about dreams from the Greeks. Emperor Augustus demanded that anyone having a dream about Rome should go the marketplace and tell it to fellow Romans. Augustus wanted to be sure he knew about every warning from the gods that might affect him or his empire.

Ancient China

The Chinese believed that people's souls could leave their bodies at night and go to the land of the dead. When they awakened, their dream stories were about things they saw and learned there. For this reason the Chinese believed it was dangerous to awaken someone suddenly, because the soul might not have returned to the body. Even today in many areas of China, alarm clocks are not popular.

Dreams and World Religions

Judaism

Judaism began about 4,000 years ago in the ancient land of Canaan. It began with a dream, or waking vision, in which God spoke to a nomad named Abraham. Like other ancient cultures, the Hebrew people believed that dreams were messages from the gods. But through Abraham's vision, they came to believe in only one God. The Jewish people did not seek dreams by sleeping in temples. They believed that trying to make dreams happen was dangerous and would result in false dreams. Instead, they waited for God to provide dreams of revelation to His chosen people in His own time.

The teachings of Judaism in the Torah tell of both waking visions and sleeping dreams. The meaning of both had to be carefully interpreted. Only people especially close to God could receive God's messages while awake. The most important dreamers were the male leaders of the Hebrew people: Abraham, Jacob, and Joseph.

The Torah contains many stories about dreams and visions from God. In the case of Joseph, the ability to interpret dreams saved his life and helped his people. When Joseph was captive in an Egyptian prison he was called before the pharaoh. The pharaoh was having strange dreams that no one could interpret. Joseph listened to the pharaoh's dreams. He told him that they were warning him that there would be a famine in Egypt, a period of seven years during which nothing would grow. If he planned now and saved food, his people would not starve. The pharaoh was so grateful that he released Joseph from prison and gave him a place of power in his palace.

Christianity

Two thousand years after Abraham, the Jewish people lived in Judea. There a woman named Mary had an amazing vision. The angel Gabriel appeared and told her that she would give birth to a baby who was the awaited Messiah, the Promised One sent to save the Jewish people. Other people had dreams about his coming birth. Joseph, Mary's fiance, dreamed that she would have a baby and the baby should be named Jesus. Three Wise Men, living in lands far from Judea, dreamed that a holy baby had been born, and they set off on their camels to find him.

A new religion was born from these waking visions and dreams in which God gave messages about the future to chosen people. To Christians the dreams came true and the promised Messiah, Jesus Christ, the Son of God, lived on earth. Today Christianity is the most widely practiced religion in the world. It's interesting that in the Bible's New Testament where Christ's teachings were recorded, there is no report that he himself talked directly about any of his own dreams or visions.

Islam

Islam is the second-largest religion in the world. Like Christianity, Islam began with the teachings of one person. Muhammad, the founder of Islam, was born in Arabia about 570 A.D. He was very interested in dreams. He believed that a dream was a conversation between a human being and God. It is said that every morning after prayers he asked his followers to come together. He encouraged them to share their dreams from the night before, and then he interpreted them. Muhammad also shared his own dreams with his followers.

At the time Muhammad lived, no difference was made between a dream during sleep and a vision while awake. The teachings of Islam are based on the messages that Muhammad received from God (Allah) in a vision. The angel Gabriel told him that God, or Allah, was all-powerful and the one and only God. Everyone was equal in Allah's eyes. He needed to tell people Allah's word. All of Muhammad's teachings and records of his visions were gathered into the Koran, the Holy Book of Islam.

The Birth of Buddha

Buddhism is one of the great religions of the world. It is the third-largest religion after Christianity and Islam. The birth of Buddha was foretold by a dream. The Buddha's mother, Queen Maya, dreamed her bed was carried by four kings to a mountain-top. There four queens greeted her with jewels and brought her to a palace of gold. A white elephant with six shining ivory tusks appeared and entered Maya's womb. She woke up to the song of a blue bird and realized that she was going to have a baby.

Dream Explorers of the Modern World

From Religion to Science

Modern scientists have made amazing progress in understanding *what* physically happens to the body when a person sleeps and dreams. However, experts have not agreed yet about *why* people dream and what dreams *mean.* In the ancient world, people were certain that dreams had meaning, contained messages from the gods, and told of future events. During the past two centuries, dream experts have continued to develop ideas about the tie between our sleeping and waking minds. For some researchers, dreams point directly to meanings that must be understood for our mental health and happiness. For others, dreaming is a random brain activity and has no meaning at all.

Sigmund Freud (1856 - 1939)

Sigmund Freud was an Austrian doctor who studied dreams in order to understand why people have mental illnesses. He found that our minds operate on two different levels. When we're awake we are conscious and can control our conscious mind by thinking. When we're asleep our conscious mind shuts down and our unconscious mind takes over. We can't control our unconscious mind. Freud believed that dreams were wishes from the dreamer's unconscious mind. These wishes are often disguised in strange pictures and stories that need to be interpreted by an trained professional. He asked his patients to try to remember and then talk about their dreams. He believed that understanding unconscious wishes expressed in dreams can help people better understand their feelings when they are awake and enable them to lead happier lives.

Carl Jung (1875 - 1961)

Carl Jung was a doctor from Switzerland who studied how people think and behave. He disagreed with Freud about what dreams mean. He agreed with him that unconscious thoughts affect people's actions when they're awake. But Jung believed that there is a deeper level in our unconscious mind that contains information about people's experiences from all of human history. This *collective consciousness,* a well of human experience and meaning, is something all humans share that stretches back to ancient times. Dreams contain universal symbols, or *archetypes,* from the collective unconscious that can be identified and understood. An archetype is not only a *picture* of something but also the *idea* of something. One archetype that Jung believed appears in people's dreams is the *hero.* The hero in ancient Hebrew tradition was David, who knocked out the giant Goliath with his slingshot and stones. The hero in your dream might be some character like Superman or Spider Woman. Understanding of the meaning of a hero is something that people have shared in their dreams for centuries.

Recent Discoveries and Theories

Scientists continue to ask questions, to experiment, and to develop theories about dreams. Some scientists, like Allan Hobson at Harvard Medical School, study the brain to find answers. He believes that a dream begins when the brain stem, a nonthinking part of the brain, sends meaningless signals to the brain's cerebral cortex. The cortex, which enables us to think, tries to give meaning to these strange pieces of information by throwing together a story. The fact that dreams are sometimes so confusing is evidence that it doesn't do a very good job. Hobson believes that while they're interesting, dreams do not have any meaning.

Some scientists think that if dreams are just the brain's way of cleaning house while we sleep, we shouldn't try so hard to remember our dreams. Other scientists are focusing on how dreaming affects learning. Research has suggested that people have an amazing ability to learn, but they can't handle all the information while awake. It's possible that important learning takes place during REM sleep to keep us in some way on-line and processing information.

Many questions are still unanswered. Where does the brain stem get its information? Why do people have the same dream over and over again if dreams mean nothing and are thrown together by chance? Why do some people have dreams that they believe warned them about something that was about to happen? What about dream stories that actually changed the world because of the meaning their dreamers found in them?

Dreams That Changed the World

Albert Einstein: The Theory of Relativity

When the famous scientist Albert Einstein was a teenager, he had a dream that led him years later to his famous discovery of the theory of relativity. In this dream he was sledding with friends. They would climb the hill, sled down, and then climb the hill again. They did this many times and were having a great time. On one run down, Einstein suddenly realized that his sled was picking up speed, going faster and faster until he believed it was getting close to the speed of light. He looked up at the stars. They were turning into colors he had never seen before. He was filled with wonder. He believed then that he had just experienced something very important. When he woke up he knew he had to understand that dream. Later in life, after he had developed the theory of relativity, he said that all his scientific work had been connected to that amazing slide down the hill in his dream.

$$E=mc^2$$

Harriet Tubman

Harriet Tubman, an escaped slave, led hundreds of other slaves north to freedom by means of the Underground Railroad. This unusual railroad didn't have tracks. It was a system of pathways and meeting stops where people offered food and shelter to escaping slaves headed north. Tubman made nineteen rescue trips to the South before the Civil War to lead people to safety. She said that she found the safe pathways through nightly dreams that showed her the safest way to go.

Abraham Lincoln

Weeks before John Wilkes Booth's bullet struck and killed President Abraham Lincoln at Ford's Theatre, Lincoln dreamed that he heard people crying. He left his bed and roamed through the White House, trying to find out where the crying was coming from. When he entered the East Room, he saw a coffin. Soldiers were guarding the coffin and many people were crying near it. In his dream Lincoln asked one of the soldiers, "Who is dead in the White House?" The soldier replied, "The President. He was killed by an assassin." A loud cry from the mourners woke Lincoln from his dream.

Elias Howe and the Sewing Machine

Elias Howe invented the sewing machine. Without the help of a dream, however, he might never have figured out how to get the thread through the cloth! One night he dreamed that he was being chased by native tribesmen carrying spears. The natives raised their spears and started to stab at the air with them. Elias Howe noticed that each spear had an eyehole through its tip. He woke up just before the spears reached his flesh. He suddenly knew that his dream had solved his problem! The needle of the sewing machine had to be like a spear that jabs up and down, with a hole in the tip that would allow the thread to pass through.

Dreaming Around the World

Introduction

Everyone dreams — people who live in icy igloos, in glittering palaces, and in sun-baked pueblos. Dreaming is something that all people share. What we think dreams mean and how important they are in our lives, however, depend on the culture we live in and the beliefs and traditions we follow.

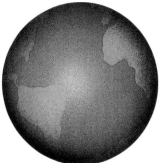

Some groups of people believe that dreams are as real as events in daily life. Some see dreams as powerful tools for learning. Others see dreams as visits from supernatural spirits who come to give messages about the future. Some believe that dream stories need to be shared for the good of the entire community. Others believe that they should be kept secret.

People around the world have developed their own ways of thinking about these mysterious movies of the night. Their beliefs about dreams are built on their own traditions, religion, and relationship to the natural world around them. Ideas about dreams are a mirror of the way each group of people lives and views the world.

Native Americans: North America

Iroquois

To the Iroquois, events in dreams are often more important than what happens to people while they're awake. They believe that there are two different kinds of dreams. In some dreams, spirits visit the dreamer with important messages for the person and the community. These dreams must be interpreted by a shaman, a tribal spiritual teacher, so that its message will be known. Other dreams are the hidden desires and wishes of the dreamer. The Iroquois believe that it is important for a person's health and well-being to try to make these dream wishes come true. If a man dreams that he is having a big dinner at his house, he should start planning to give such a dinner as soon as he wakes up.

Hopi

The Hopi believe that when you have a good dream, you should hold it in your heart and tell no one until it comes true. However, if you have a bad dream, you should discuss it with others. Talking about it will help you get rid of it.

Cherokee

The Cherokee traditionally believe that it's a good idea to make sure that what happens in a dream doesn't harm you while awake. If a Cherokee man dreams he has been bitten by a snake, when he wakes up he must get treated for a snake bite immediately.

Navajo

Dreams are very important to the Navajo people. They believe that both good and bad dreams are placed in the head of the dreamer by gods, spirits, and animals. Some dreams are warnings and must be understood for everyone's safety. To learn a dream's meaning the Navajo don't share the dream with family and friends. Instead, they go to a dream teacher or interpreter. The teacher can help them explore the cause of the dream. They can also tell them which rituals and ceremonies to perform to stop anything bad from happening.

Navajo Song to Straighten a Bad Dream

All is beautiful where I dream.
All is beautiful where I dream.
I dream amid the dawn and all is beautiful.
I dream amid the white corn and all is beautiful.
I dream amid the beautiful goods and all is beautiful.
I dream amid all the pollens and all is beautiful.
I dream that all is beautiful.

Ojibwa

Children in the Ojibwa community learn early that dreams are important to their education. They are encouraged to try very hard to remember their dreams. During dreams the Ojibwa spirits or gods visit them and help them learn important things for their lives. They believe that a good life is possible because humans help each other and non-human spirits come during dreams to teach and give advice.

Zuni

The Zuni people of New Mexico regularly share their dreams with family and friends. However, they consider it bad luck to brag about a good-news dream until the events have come true. Sometimes years go by before a dream is shared. As a result, the Zuni share dreams that are more sad than happy. The Zuni also believe that dreams can help people create beautiful artwork. Zuni potters have reported that during a dream they were given a new design to paint on their pots.

Paiute

The Paiute people of the Southwest believe that dreams can be the cause of an illness. A dream-caused sickness may affect the dreamer or even a close relative. People who are sick are asked questions about their recent dreams to help treat them.

Mexico, Central and South America

Raramuri Indians: Mexico

The Raramuri people usually sleep for just a few hours, wake up, and then fall asleep again. Each time they wake up they talk about their dreams with family and friends to remember and understand them.

Quiche Maya: Guatemala

The Quiche believe that the gods or ancestors come to a sleeper's body and awaken the soul. The soul is then free to leave the body and wander around in the world meeting the souls of other people and animals. When the dreamers wake up, their dreams must be reported and examined for information about their nighttime travels.

Kuna Indians: San Blas Islands - Panama

The Kuna Indians regularly report their dreams to others. If they believe they've had an important dream, they can report it at a community meeting. They believe that dreams can have an affect on daily life, and they often see dreams as warnings. If a Kuna man dreams about a fish hook, he might be excused from work that day because he is at high risk for a snakebite.

Mapuche Indians: Chile

The Mapuche people share dreams with their families every day. They talk about them and believe that this helps them solve problems. They only go to the shaman or spiritual leader with a dream if the family can't figure out its meaning.

Parintinin Indians: Brazil

The Parintinin Indians, who live by the Amazon River in Brazil, have created a special language and way to talk about their dreams. Dreams are so important to the dreamer and the tribe that dream stories have to be told correctly and in a special way.

Quechua Indians: Peru

The Quechua people believe that if people getting up from sleep stand on their left foot first, it means that they had a dream in which a bad omen or message for the future appeared.

Africa

Saudi Arabia

Arab people have traditionally believed that when people dream their souls float over everything they want to have in real life. When they wake up they remember the amazing pictures from their nighttime journey. If their soul is pure, the pictures will speak the truth. If their soul is not pure, the pictures will fool and mislead them.

Berti: Republic of the Sudan

The Berti people would rather not remember their dreams when they wake up in the morning. If they do wake up with dream images on their minds, they keep them private and don't talk about them. If they remember a powerful dream picture that can't be ignored, the tribe will interpret the dream according to traditional tribal signs and symbols. The Berti believe that the wind dream symbol is a sign that something bad will happen in the future.

Zambia

Zambian shamans are powerful spiritual dream teachers. They use information from dreams to tell people about their physical health. By interpreting dream images they believe they can tell what is wrong with people without even examining them.

Southeast Asia and Australia

Aborigines: Australia

The Aborigines have lived in Australia for more than 40,000 years. There are more than 500 different tribal groups. As a people they believe that the dreaming and waking worlds are both real. There is no difference. Dreams are especially important because they allow people to get power, information, and advice from their ancestors.

Senoi: Malaysia

The Senoi people live in a peaceful, nonviolent way. They do not want their children to be negatively affected by violent and upsetting dreams. They believe that children can be trained to stop bad dreams and turn them into positive experiences. From the earliest age, Senoi children learn that dreams are valuable and important, and they are taught that they can control their dreams. During nightmares they can face their fears and stop the terrible things that are happening. Without waking up, they can turn a bad dream into a good one.

Kiwai: Papua New Guinea

The Kiwai people worry about sick people in the village who go to sleep and dream. They believe that they might be taken by evil spirits while dreaming. To make sure that doesn't happen, they sit by the bedsides of the sick and wake them up several times during the night.

Dreams That Inspire

Introduction

Where do creative people get their ideas for new stories, paintings, theories, songs, movies, and projects? Throughout history, one of the places that artists of all types have found inspiration is in their own dreams.

The way dreams put together things that don't seem to relate makes people think in a different way. The way dreams point to meaning, but hold it slightly out of sight, makes people wonder and try their own ways of making sense of dream movies. The unusual and mysterious world that dreams live in tug at a creative person's imagination. Because of it, often something new in the world is born.

A Nightmare Comes to the Rescue

Scottish author Robert Louis Stevenson can thank his nightmares for his fame and fortune. At one point in his life he badly needed money. He tried hard to think of a good story to write, but he just couldn't think of anything exciting. For many days he thought and thought with no luck. Then one night he dreamed a scene from a story. In it he saw a gentleman being chased through the streets as a criminal. All at once, this Dr. Jekyll swallowed a magic powder. In front of the amazed and terrified people chasing him, he turned into the evil monster, Mr. Hyde. Stevenson had the creative idea he needed. He woke up and wrote the rest of the story which became the famous novel, *The Strange Case of Dr. Jekyll and Mr. Hyde.*

The Birth of Frankenstein

One night in 1816, Mary Shelley was telling ghost stories with her husband and some friends, all of whom were writers. At the end of the evening they decided that each would try to write a horror story. Mary Shelley went to bed and dreamed about a strange who was made out of body pieces by a "pale student." This horrible-looking, pieced-together man was "stretched out," and a machine was used to awaken him. When she woke up she knew that this monster that frightened her in her dream would also terrify her readers. She sat down to write her horror story. In 1818 she published *Frankenstein,* one of the most famous scary stories of all time.

Painting the Flag

In the early 1950s, Jasper Johns worked at arranging window displays for New York City stores. This was how he earned money, but he was really a painter. One night he dreamed about painting the American flag. It was a dream he couldn't forget. He decided to paint the flag just as he had painted it in his dream. His American flag painting became famous, and today he is one of the most admired and successful modern artists.

The Perfect Swing

Dreams can even improve golf scores. A story in the *San Francisco Chronicle* newspaper on June 27, 1974, tells how a dream helped professional golfer Jack Nicklaus break out of a terrible period of miserable golf scores. No matter how hard he tried, he continued to lose. Then, one night, he dreamed he was holding the golf club differently and as a result swinging it just right. He told the newspaper reporter: "When I came to the golf course yesterday morning, I tried it the way I did in my dream and it worked. . . . I feel kind of foolish admitting it, but it really happened in a dream." His golf scores got better from that day on.

The Snake That Changed Chemistry

Friedrich Kekulé was a chemist who worked to understand molecules. He just couldn't figure out how they fit together. Then, one night, he had a dream about a snake curling around until it grabbed its tail in its mouth and made a complete circle. When he woke up he knew this was the clue he had been looking for to solve his problem. He went on to discover the ringed structure or shape of the benzene molecule. It was a discovery that changed the study of chemistry. He was so excited by the power of dreams to solve problems, he told other scientists: *Let us learn to dream, gentlemen, and then we may perhaps learn to know the truth.*

Waking at the Right Time

Salvador Dali was a famous member of a group of modern artists who decided to paint the strange pictures they saw in their dreams as a way of describing a new reality different from daily life. They called themselves *surrealists.* Dali used to make himself dream by falling asleep in a chair with a bright light on. He would put his chin in his hand and jerk himself awake soon after he started dreaming. By waking up during REM sleep, he found he could remember his dream images and paint them.

Dream Movies

Movies make it possible to enter another world through pictures and sound. Many filmmakers have been inspired by dreams and use dreams in their films. Here's a list of popular dream movies for kids. Some of them are based on famous stories.

A Christmas Carol   *The Neverending Story*

Alice in Wonderland   *The Wizard of Oz*

The Navigator

The Beatles

Paul McCartney said he first heard the tune for the famous Beatles hit "Yesterday" in a dream.

Learning From Your Dreams

Introduction

Everyone dreams, but not everyone tries to remember his or her dreams. It takes some time and effort, but many people believe it's worth it. Much can be learned from these strange movies of the night. A dream may give you ideas about how to solve a problem. It might give you inspiration for a story, a poem, or a drawing. It may help you better understand your feelings.

Dreams are like messages to yourself from yourself. They are expressed in a private language or code from your own experiences and feelings. Because they are so personal, you probably are the best person to decide what your own dreams mean. Like any puzzle, your dreams require your attention, time, and effort to find the clues and work out their hidden patterns. The messages you uncover may amaze and inspire you.

Remembering Your Dreams

1. Get enough rest. When you're overtired you will sleep deeper and have a more difficult time remembering your dreams.

2. Before you go to sleep, review what happened during the day. Think about the things that are important to you. Write out a dream question about one of those things. Repeat it to yourself as you drift off to sleep. Tell yourself that you will remember your dreams when you wake up.

3. Don't set an alarm. Being startled by the sound of an alarm clock going off usually zaps a dream right out of your memory.

4. Don't jump right out of bed! Lie still when you wake up. Even stretching and turning over can sometimes make dream memories vanish into thin air. Keep your eyes closed for a few moments and think about the dream from beginning to end. Ask yourself questions about it: Where was I? Who was there? What did it look like? What happened? What did I do? Did anyone say anything? How did I feel?

Recording Your Dreams

People who want to learn from their night movies keep dream supplies by their beds to help them remember and record their dreams.

Dream Book: Keep a notebook or dream book and pen by your bed. Write down all you can remember about your dream as quickly as you can. Think of it as a movie and write as many details as you can about the setting, the characters, and the story action. Write down any feelings you had during the dream or about it after waking up. Don't worry if it doesn't make sense. Just try to list as many details as possible. These could include names, people, numbers, words said, sounds, smells, colors, events, and strong feelings.

Flashlight: You may want to keep a flashlight next to your dream book. Sometimes, when you wake up in the middle of the night, your last dream will be clearest in your memory. A flashlight helps you avoid waking everyone else up while you write in your dream book.

Audiotape player: If you would rather talk about your dream than write about it, put a tape player by your bed.

Working and Playing With Your Dreams

Mind Play: To draw meaning from your dreams, let your mind play with the main parts of your dream story. Take each important object, person, event, or feeling you can remember and write it in big letters on a separate piece of paper. Focus on each one and let your mind play with all the things this item reminds you of. Fill the page with other words, phrases, or even drawings you associate with this element of your dream. Sometimes things you see in your dream don't make any sense until you think about what they remind you of in your waking life.

Free Write: Think about your dream. Put your pen on your paper and just keep writing about your dream until you fill up a whole page (and more!). Don't let your pen stop, even if you have to write silly words between thoughts. This free-write activity will help draw dream memories from your unconscious mind.

Quick Sketch: Think about the images or pictures in your dream. As quickly as you can, make sketches of each one. Don't worry about the quality of the drawing — just get the pictures down on paper. Create whole scenes as you remember them.

Feeling Phrases: Make a quick list of all the feelings you had during or about your dream. Sometimes dreams exaggerate the feelings you've had the day before. They may also be strong feelings you can't express while awake. Short phrases or descriptions of your dream emotions can help you figure out what your mind is trying to tell you.

Dream Gallery

What if I dream I'm a fish?

This Dream Gallery is not intended to tell you exactly what each image in your dream means. Dream interpretation is much more difficult than that and very personal. Some experts specialize in helping people find meaning from their dreams. Because dreams are created by your unique mind and experiences, however, you are likely to be your own best dream expert.

Although they don't always agree, dream experts try to give people information that will help them make sense of their dreams. Go into any bookstore and you'll see shelves of books with dream definitions for every object or type of event. For example, most dream books explain that when you dream about a house, it stands for your own body. But it's never that easy. What if you dream that the house is falling down? What if it changes into the home of the richest person in the world? What if you're in the kitchen and there are ice cubes all over the floor? What if you're in the attic that is full of giant fish and suddenly you become one? What if you open the door and enter a new room in the house that you didn't even know was there? What if that door is red? You have to look to your own experiences and feelings to solve each dream puzzle.

Types of Dreams

Everyday Dreams: Dream experts agree that we usually dream about things and people that we care about when we're awake: school, friends, family, home, pets, and activities.

Frightening Dreams: You don't need to have a terrible nightmare to dream about frightening things. Inside many dreams there are moments when scary things happen. Two-thirds of our dreams are anxious rather than happy.

Half True Dreams: You dream that you are wearing a big, heavy, furry hat. It's starting to itch. You wake up to find your cat is asleep wrapped around your head. Actions or feelings in your dream can be influenced by what is happening around you as you sleep.

Problem-Solving Dreams: Some dream experts believe that we work out our problems in our dreams. Our dreams don't give us answers —they give us information to use to solve problems. Examine your dreams for information that might help you with a current problem.

Future Dreams: Some dreams are about things that haven't happened yet. They seem to warn you about future events. Often when you have something coming up that you don't want to go to, you'll dream about it days before it is to happen. A scheduled appointment with the dentist or an upcoming speech you have to give in front of the class can bring on anxious dreams about the future.

Dream Gallery Definitions

Apple Tree: Good luck and good things to come from hard work

Avalanche: Feeling overwhelmed

Balloon: Release of feelings or creative ideas

Baby: Something new in your life, or feeling helpless and needing to ask for help

Being Late: Anxiety about something you need to do but have been putting off

Boat: Family or home life

Book: Knowledge and wisdom

Bridges: Travel, change, or something that brings together two separate things

Cage: The need to escape, feeling confined

Cat: Independence and power

Cemetery: Sadness, grief, or the past

Chased: Running from a problem or situation that is too frightening

Cliff: A problem that needs to be solved

Clock: Anxiety about not being on top of things

Clown: Something happy and funny about you, or the need to disguise sad feelings

Curtains: Hiding something from yourself or others

Dolphins: Message between our conscious and unconscious minds, or between our thoughts and emotions

Door: New opportunity

Dynamite: Anger or strong explosive feelings

Earthquake: Life crises or major change

Elephant: Something very important or a huge task

Falling: Something in your life is out of control; you feel frightened and powerless

Fence: Something in the way or offering protection

Flying: Feeling happy and relieved because something difficult has passed

Fog: Feeling lost or confused

Gold: A bright event in the future

Green: Prosperity and healing

Hands: Building, healing, praying

Key: A secret

Lion: Daring, strength, leadership

Mask: Presenting a false self to others to protect yourself

Money: Self-worth or self-esteem

Monsters: Fear of being dominated or hurt

Moon: Your inner feelings and the ways you express them

Octopus: A relationship or situation that is entangling you

Pilot: Ability to rise above a situation or problem

Rainbow: Happiness

River: Passing time

Rocket: Plans about to take off

Test Taking: Feeling unprepared for a challenge you need to face

Tornado: Problems or situations that make you feel overwhelmed and out of control

Visitor: New changes, information, or feelings

Water: Unconscious mind

Waves: Emotions

Whale: Something in your life that is too big to handle

Wind: Change or need for a change

Dream Resources

Books for Kids

Emert, Phyllis Raybin. *The Book of Nightmares: A Fiendish Guide to Your Scary Dreams.* Los Angeles, CA: Lowell House, 1997.

MacGregor, Trish & Rob. *The Everything Dreams Book.* Holbrook, MA: Adams Media Corporation, 1998.

Mayle, Peter. *Sweet Dreams and Monsters.* New York: Harmony Books, 1986.

Policoff, Stephen Phillip. *The Dreamer's Companion: A Young Person's Guide to Understanding Dreams and Using Them Creatively.* Chicago, IL: Chicago Review Press, 1997.

Reid, Lori. *Sweet Dreamer: A Guide to Understanding Your Dreams.* Boston, MA: Element Books, 1999.

General Resources (Parents)

Golbin, Alexander Z. *The World of Children's Sleep: Parent's Guide to Understanding Children and Their Sleep Problems.* Salt Lake City, UT: Michaelis Medical Pub. Corp., 1995.

Parker, Julia & Derek. *The Complete Book of Dreams.* New York: Dorling Kindersley, 1995.

Siegel, Alan, & Bulkeley, Kelly. *Dreamcatching: Every Parent's Guide to Exploring and Understanding Children's Dreams and Nightmares.* New York: Three Rivers Press, 1998.

Van de Castle, Robert L. *Our Dreaming Mind.* New York: Ballantine Books, 1994.

Index

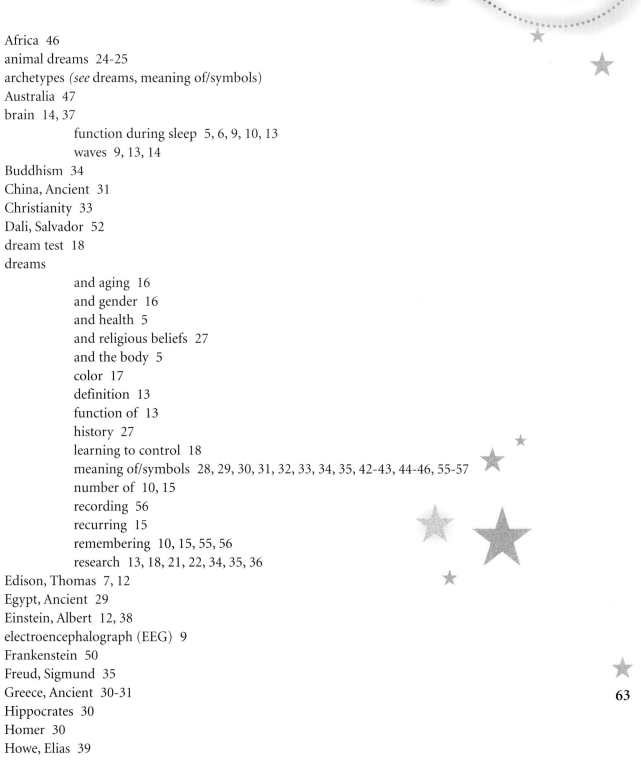